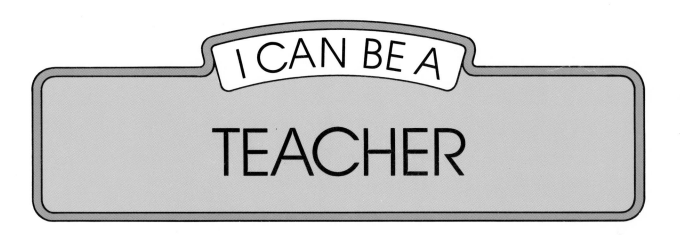

I CAN BE A

TEACHER

By Beatrice Beckman

Prepared under the direction of Robert Hillerich, Ph.D.

CHILDRENS PRESS ™
CHICAGO

Library of Congress Cataloging in Publication Data

Beckman, Beatrice.
 I can be a teacher.
 Includes index.

 Summary: Describes in simple terms the training and
duties of a teacher.
 1. Teachers—Vocational guidance—Juvenile literature.
 2. Teaching—Juvenile literature. [1. Teachers. 2. Occupations]
I. Title. II. Title: Teacher.
LB1775.B412 1985   371.1'0023   84-23236
ISBN 0-516-01843-4

PICTURE DICTIONARY

BASIC SUBJECTS

reading   math   science

SPECIAL SUBJECTS

art   music   physical education

SCIENCE TEACHER

plants   sound waves

college

hibernation   electricity

lessons

CLASSROOM

students

class
grade

student teacher

bulletin board

MATERIALS

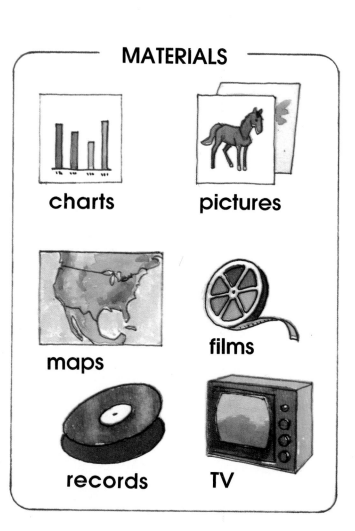

charts

pictures

maps

films

records

TV

assemblies

clubs

records

Reading teacher

Math teacher

Art teacher

Teaching is a very special job. Teachers help other people get ready to live and work in the world.

There are many kinds of teachers. Some teach basic subjects such as reading, math, and science. Others teach special subjects such as art, music, and physical education.

BASIC SUBJECTS

reading   math   science

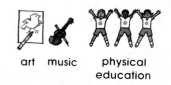

art   music   physical education

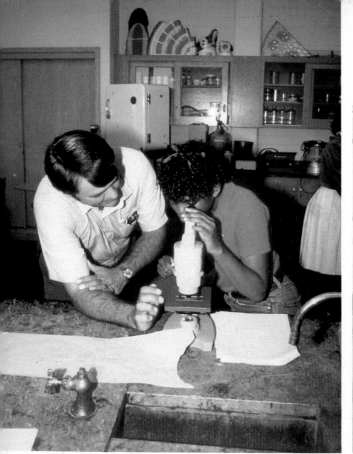 

Most teachers work in
schools. Sometimes they
work with large groups,
sometimes with small
groups. Sometimes they
help one person at a
time.

Many teachers stay with
the same students all
day. All the students are
in the same grade. These
teachers usually teach all
the basic subjects to their
students.

Music teacher

Gym teacher

Dance teacher

Sometimes these teachers teach special subjects, too. They teach art, music, and physical education. In some schools the students have other teachers for special subjects.

Some teachers teach only one or two subjects. This may sound easy, but it isn't.

The computer teacher (left) and math teacher (right) teach students from different grades.

Students from different grades come to these teachers. The teachers teach a different part of the subject to each grade. For example, a science teacher might

Students learn about baby chickens.

teach third graders about plants, fourth graders about hibernation, fifth graders about sound waves, and sixth graders about electricity. All in a single day.

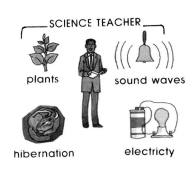

SCIENCE TEACHER

plants

sound waves

hibernation

electricty

College students must study hard.

Becoming a teacher is not easy. Teachers must finish at least four years of college. People who want to be teachers must study hard. They must learn about the subjects they will teach. They must know how people learn. They must learn the best ways to present ideas to their students.

college

Student teachers work with classroom teachers
in order to learn more about their jobs.

Have you ever had a student teacher in your room? Student teachers are usually in their last year of college. They are practice teachers. They work in schools with classroom teachers. The student teachers do many of the things they will do if they become full-time teachers.

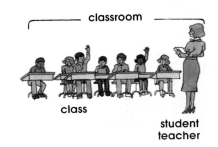

Globes (left) and models (right) are used to teach.

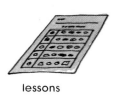
lessons

Student teachers find
out that teachers do not
just teach from books.
They use many different
things to make their
lessons clear and
interesting.

Pictures (left) and maps (right) can help students learn.

Teachers use special
materials when they
work. They use pictures,
charts, and maps. They
show films. They play
records. They have their
students watch lessons on
TV.

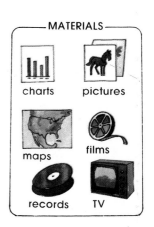

Teachers make some of the special materials they use. They borrow some from libraries. They rent or buy others from companies.

Collecting teaching materials takes time and work, but it is worth it. Teachers want to make learning interesting and fun.

Teachers make their rooms places where students want to learn. The teachers plan decorations and activities. They put examples of the students' work on bulletin boards. They often ask students to help them.

bulletin board

Teachers do more than teach subjects. They also have other jobs.

They may work on the playground before or after school. Some teachers have playground duty during the lunch hour.

A teacher's day does not end when school is out.

Teachers usually take
turns being on lunchroom
duty. Sometimes they are
also on duty in the halls.
Their job is to care for
the safety of the students.

Teacher and class on a field trip (left). Drama clubs (right)
are usually run by a teacher after school hours.

Teachers often plan
special assemblies. They
also work with school
clubs. They take students
on field trips.

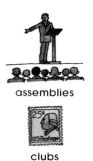

assemblies

clubs

Teachers prepare lesson plans (left) and grade papers (right) after school hours.

records

A teacher's day does not end when school is out. Teachers still have work to do. They must mark papers. They must plan lessons. They must keep records. Some records are for the school. Some are for parents.

Teachers meetings are held after school.

Teachers must go to
teachers' meetings and
PTA meetings. They must
be in school on parents'
nights. They often
are asked to work with
neighborhood groups.

As you can see, it takes a very special kind of person to be a teacher. Do you like helping others to learn? Are you patient? Can you explain things well? Are you willing to work hard?

Did you answer *yes* to all the questions? If so, perhaps you should think about becoming a teacher. Study hard in

school. Watch your
teachers. Learn what they
do. Work with others
when you get the
chance. Then maybe
one day you can be a
teacher.

WORDS YOU SHOULD KNOW

assembly (uh • SEM • blee)—special program of entertainment or instruction for which students are gathered together

basic (BAY • sik)—forming the basis, or foundation

borrow (BAR • oh)—to take or have something for a certain length of time before returning it

college (KAHL • ij)—a school for students who have graduated from high school and want to learn more

duty (DOO • tee)—work that must be done because it is part of one's job or position

examples (ex • AM • pils)—sample things that stand for other things in the same group

field trip (FEELD TRIP)—a visit by students to see something they are studying, such as a fire station, a farm, or a hospital

full-time (FULL-TYME)—the whole time for working, as opposed to part-time

idea (eye • DEE • uh)—something thought up in your mind that you may try to use

learn (LERN)—to get new facts, new skills, or the ability to do something new

neighborhood (NAY • ber • hood)—the part of a town or city around your home

patient (PAY • shunt)—being calm and able to wait

PTA —abbreviation for Parent-Teacher Association

records (REK • erds)—papers and facts that are saved so they can be looked up later

rent (RENT)—to pay money to be able to use a thing for a certain length of time

safety (SAYF • tee)—being safe from getting hurt or injured

special (SPESH • il)—not the usual thing; out of the ordinary

student teacher (STOOD • ent TEE • cher)—college student who works as a practice teacher in a class taught by a regular classroom teacher

subjects (SUB • jekts)—the divisions of learning; different classes of information or knowledge

willing (WILL • ing)—ready; something one has chosen to do

INDEX

PHOTO CREDITS
  © Tony Freeman—22 (2 photos), 29
Image Finders:
  © Bob Skelly—6 (top left), 14 (bottom), 26 (right)
Nawrocki Stock Photo:
  © Larry Brooks—27
  © Donner—25 (right)
  © William S. Nawrocki—4 (top and bottom left), 7, 8 (top and bottom right),
    14 (top), 17 (left)
  © Steve Sumner—24, 25 (left)
  © Jim Whitmer—6 (right), 8 (bottom left)
  © Jim Wright—12
Journalism Services:
  © Richard Derk—Cover, 11
© Lynn M. Stone—4 (bottom right), 10 (2 photos), 16 (2 photos), 17 (right),
    19 (2 photos), 20 (2 photos), 21, 26 (left)

ABOUT THE AUTHOR

Beatrice Beckman is a former teacher of English. She later turned to educational publishing where she was the editorial director of language arts and early childhood programs. A native New Yorker, Ms. Beckman lives in Chicago where she works as a free-lance writer and editor.